Kids Draw 100 Things

What you'll find inside

Chick

Football

Fish

Fox

Cactus

Fairy

Umbrella

Dinosaur

Unicorn

Bow Tie

Cat

Boot

Pencil

Apple

Sailboat

Ice Cream

Cupcake

Flower

Lollipop

Puppy

Sheep

Christmas Tree

Rain Cloud

Snail

Piggy Bank

Space Rocket

Chocolate

Basketball

Mermaid

Tomato

Crab

Pie

Snowman

Watermelon Slice

Burger

Planet

Knight

Electric Bulb

Candy Cane

UFO

Butterfly

Witch

Pizza

Bee

Candy

Turtle

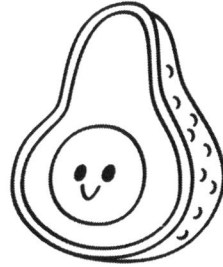

Avocado

Bat

Cherry

Worm

Cake Slice

Race Car

Orange

Clown

Crown

Teapot

Shooting Star

Pineapple

Elf

Paint Brush

Banana

Teddy Bear

Letter

Dolphin

Shovel

The Sun

Girl

Present

The Moon

T-Shirt

Edamame

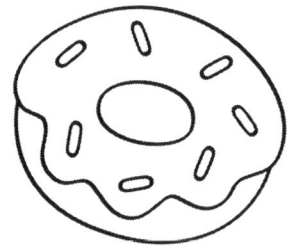

Donut

Toothbrush

Hot Air Balloon

Owl

Castle

Boat

Boy

Jam Jar

Victory Cup

Tennis Racket

Birthday Cake

Duck Toy

Beach Hat

Mountain

Mouse

Cap

Carrot

Whale

Diamond

Accordion

Crocodile

Radish

Bird

Airplane

Ghost

Princess

Mushroom

Trumpet

The Art Teacher

Useful Tips

Hello There! Let's have fun and draw together!

• Have your pencils and paper ready!

• Start with light strokes, don't press too hard on the paper!

• Erase any mistakes or shaky lines

• When you're happy with your drawing, darken or thicken the lines

• Follow the drawing steps, one by one, and before you know it, you'll create amazing drawings

• You can add color and bring it to life!

Remember, practice makes perfect, so keep drawing and have fun with your artwork!

Chick

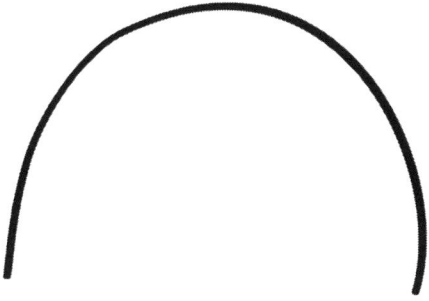 

Football

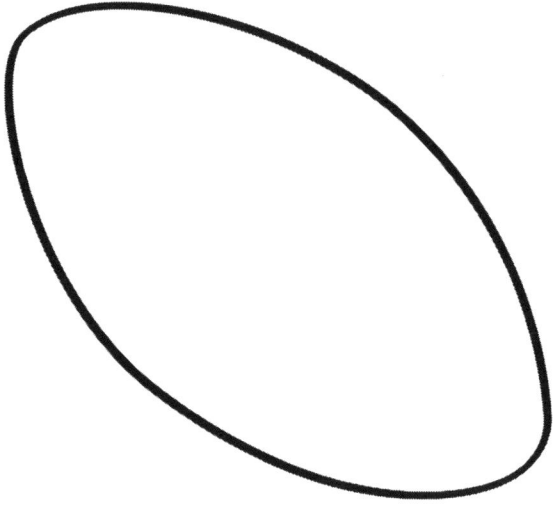
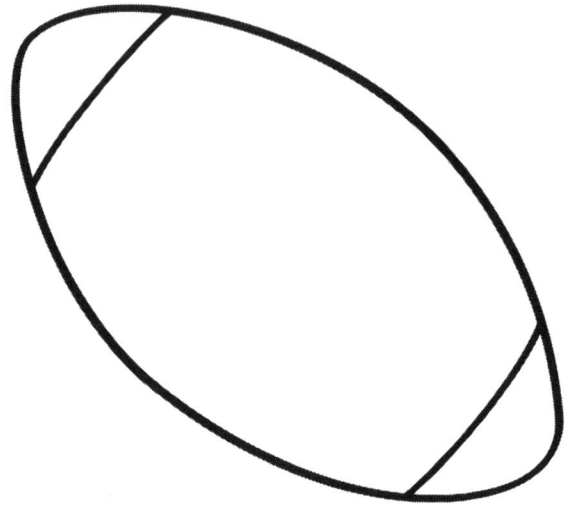
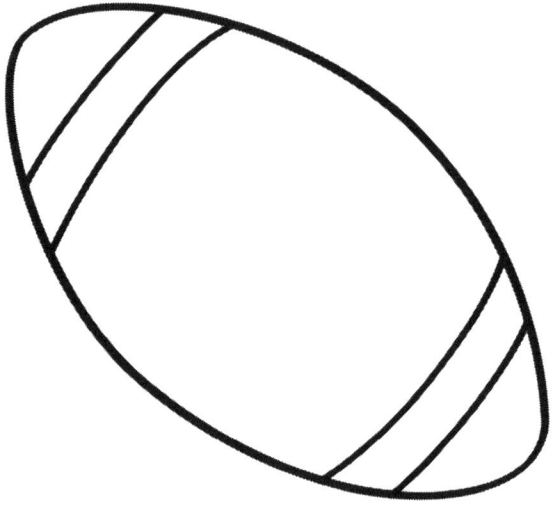
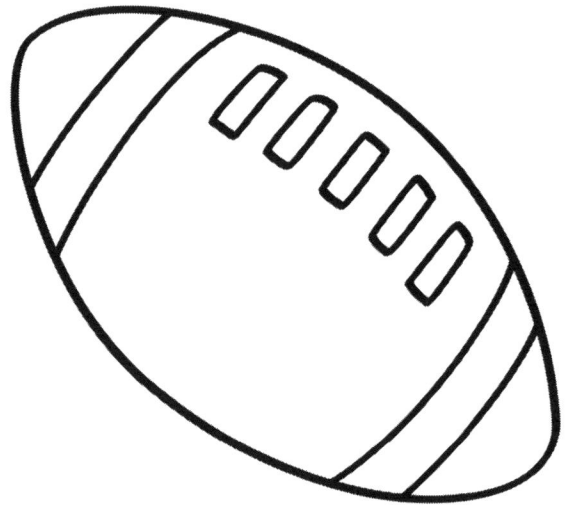

Fish

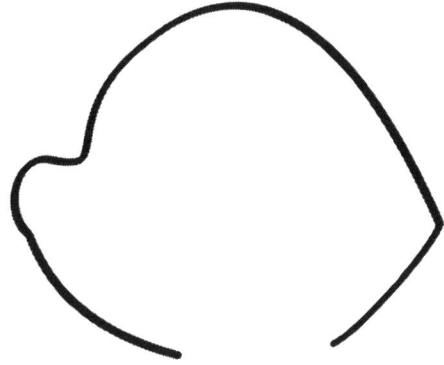
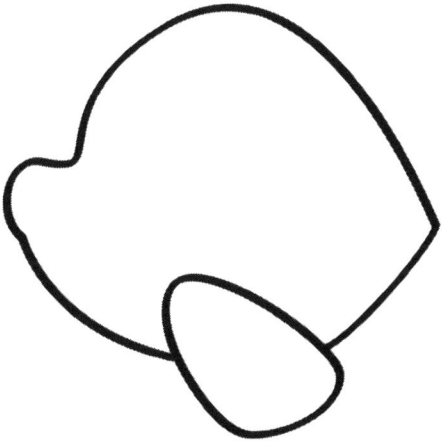

Fox

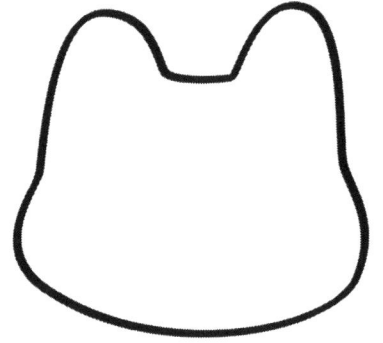
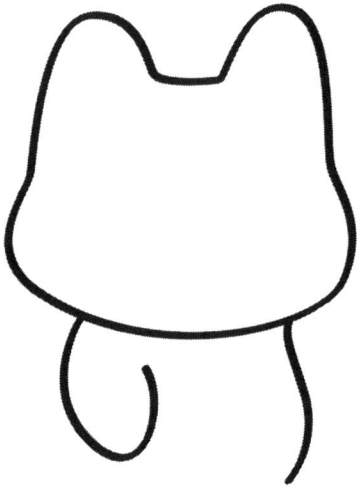

Cactus

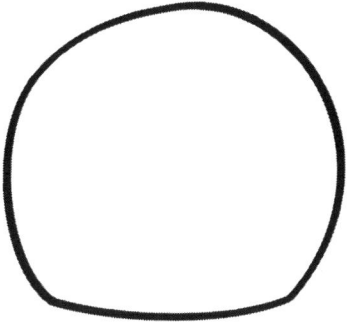

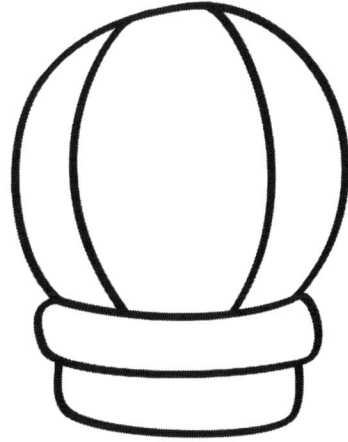

Fairy

Umbrella

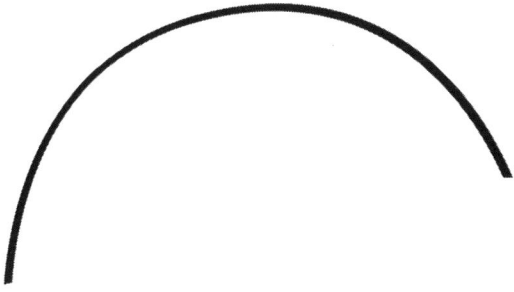 

Dinosaur

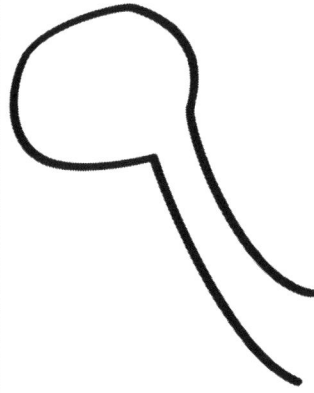
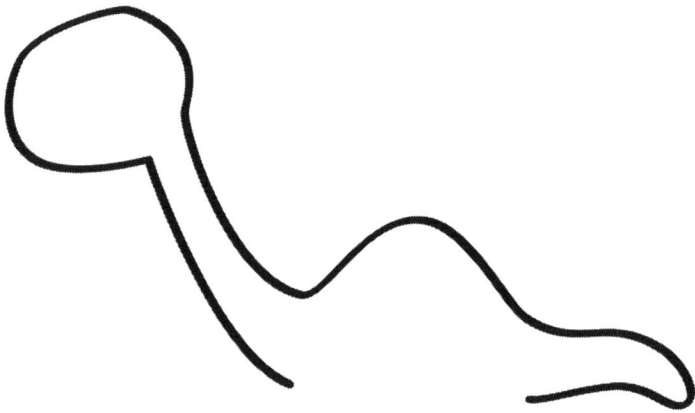

Unicorn

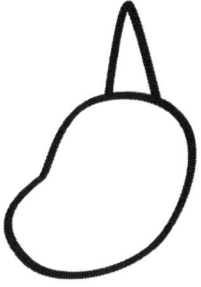

Bow Tie

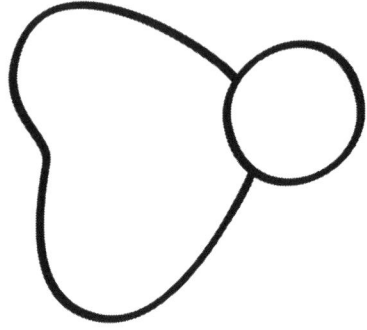
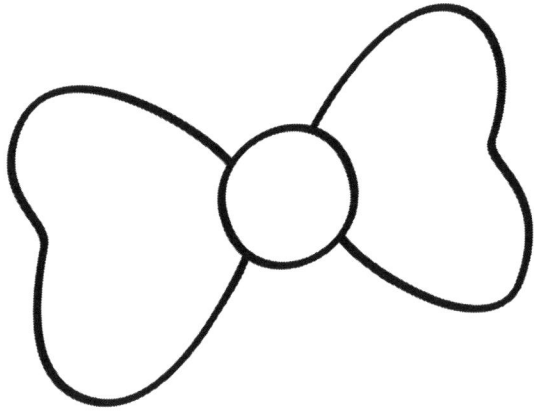

Cat

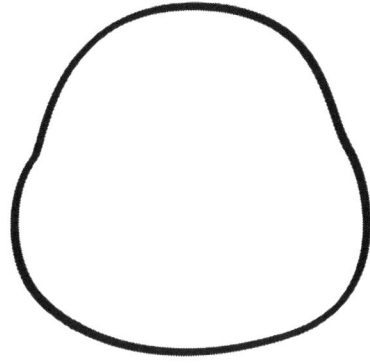

Boot

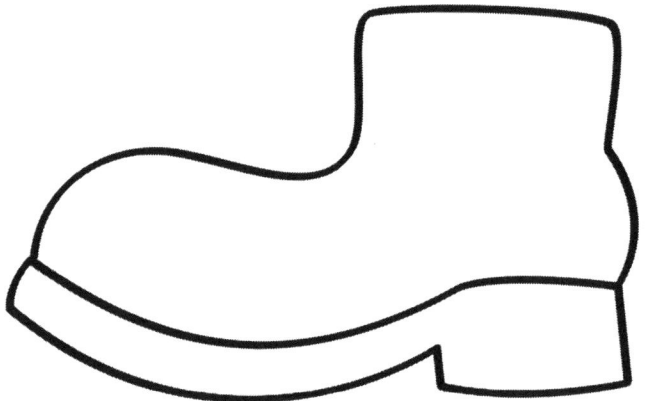

Pencil

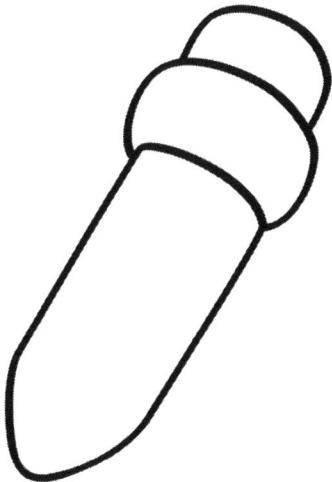

Apple

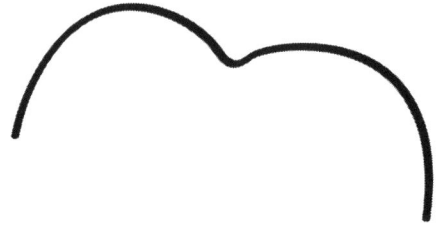

Sailboat

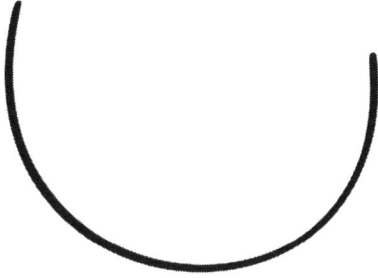
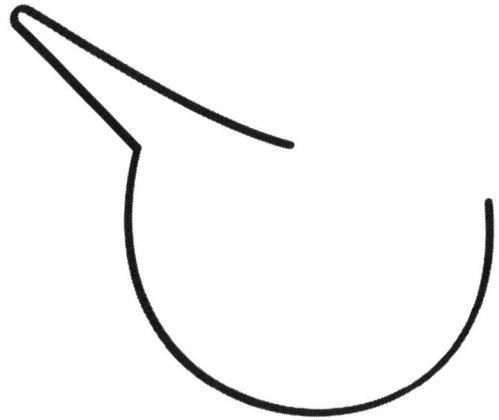

Ice Cream

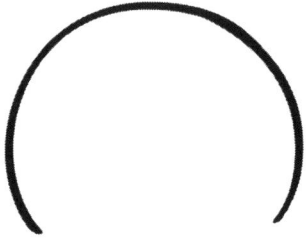

Cupcake

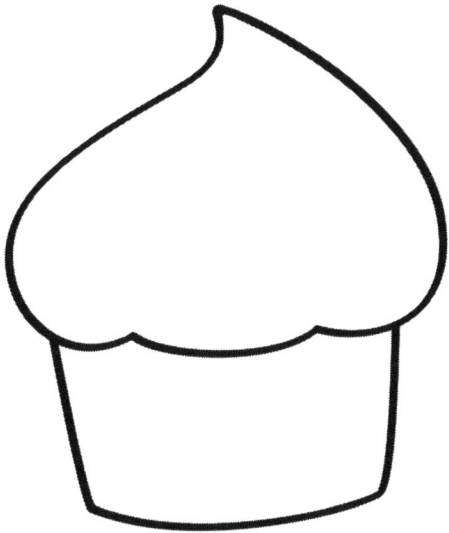

Flower

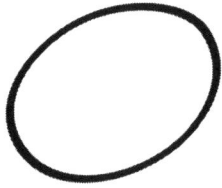

Lollipop

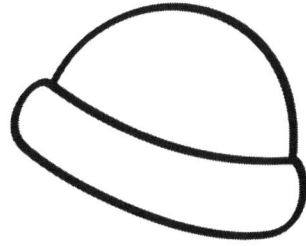

Puppy

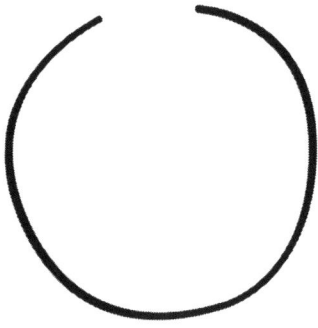
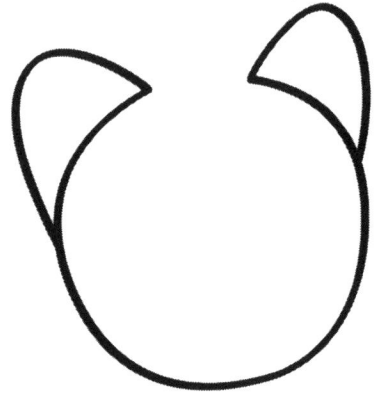

Sheep

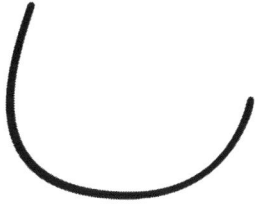
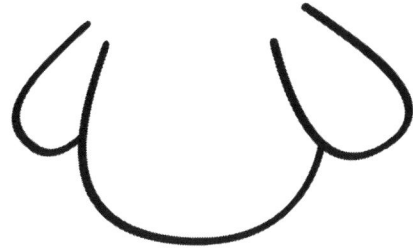

Christmas Tree

Rain Cloud

Snail

Piggy Bank

Space Rocket

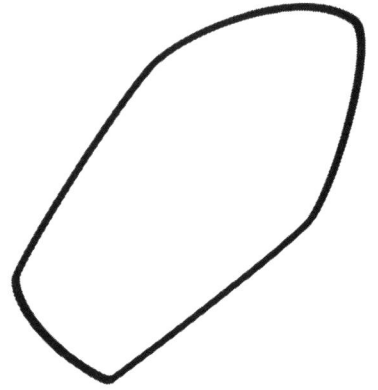

Chocolate

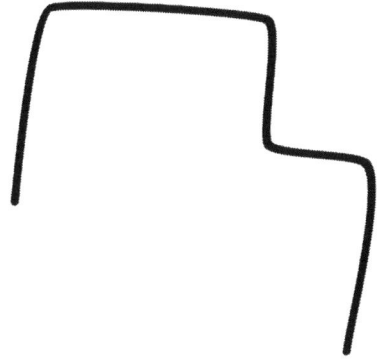
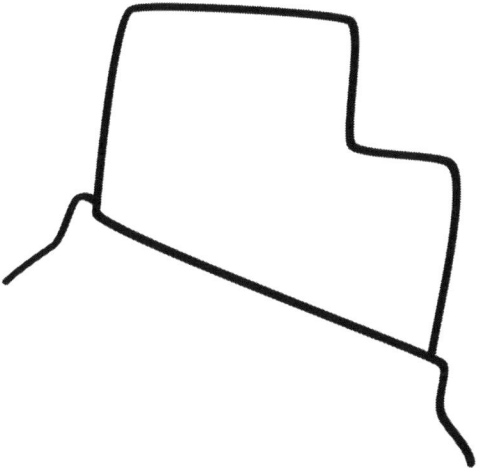
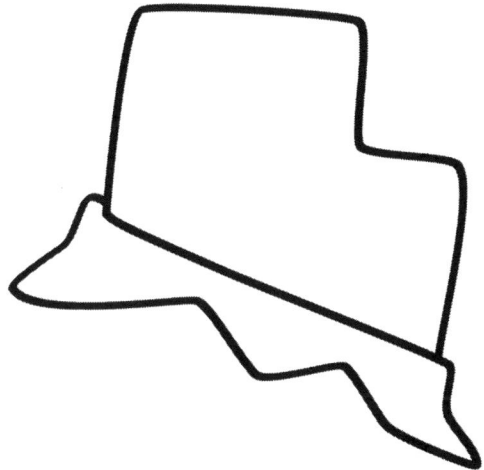
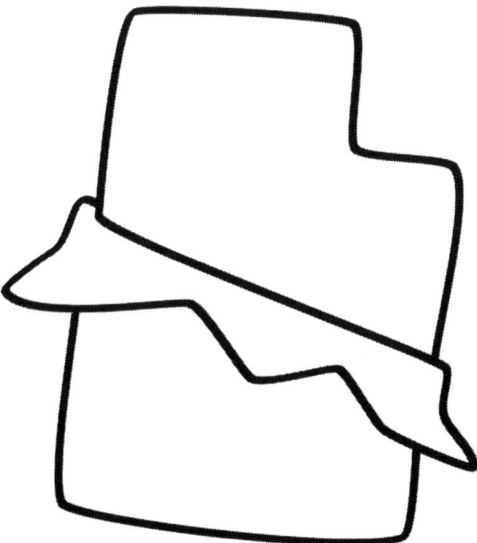

Basketball

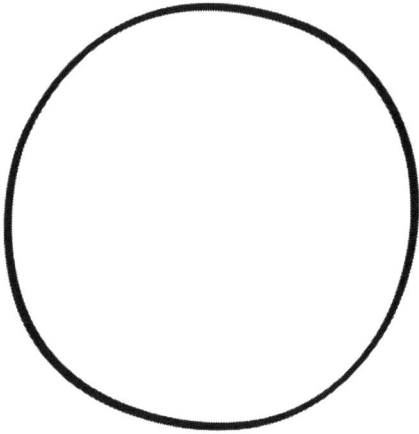
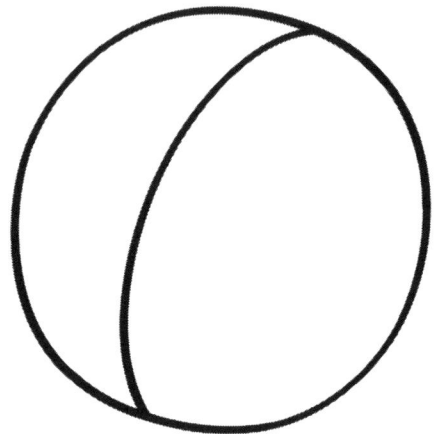

Mermaid

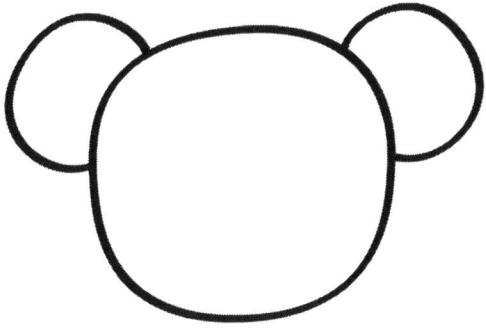

Tomato

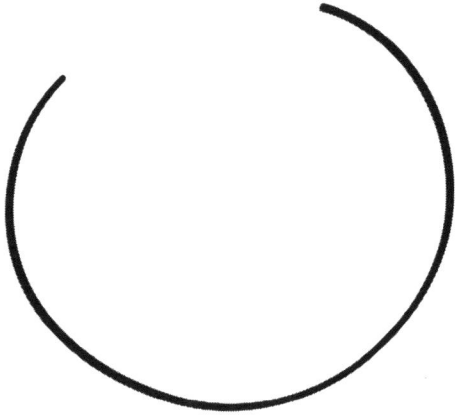

Crab

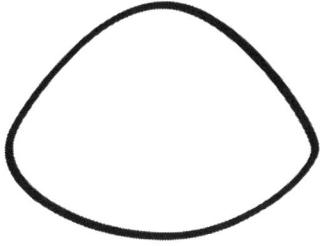

pie

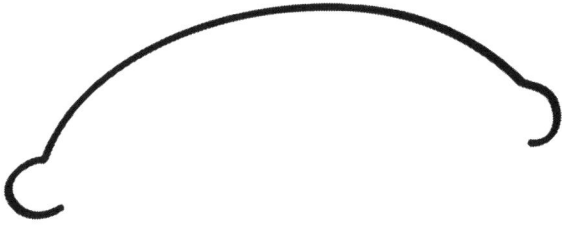

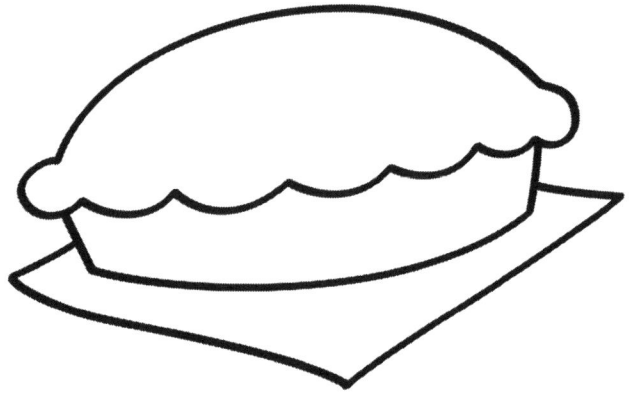

Snowman

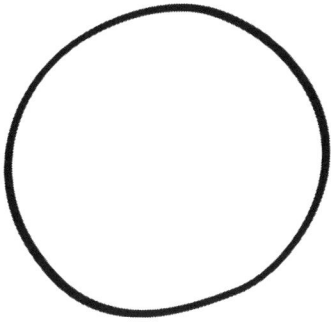

Watermelon Slice

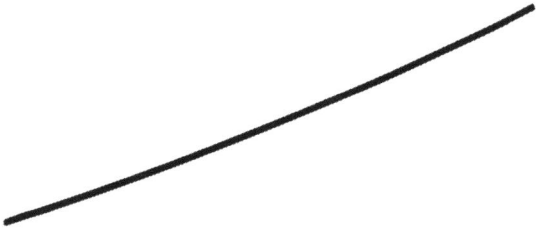

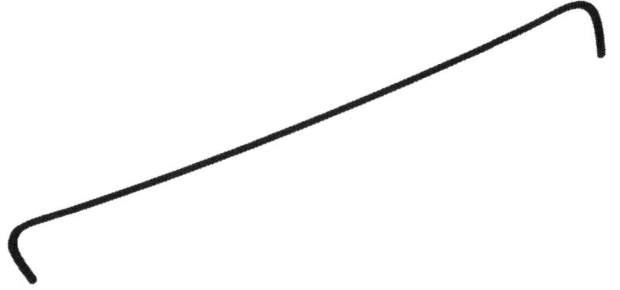

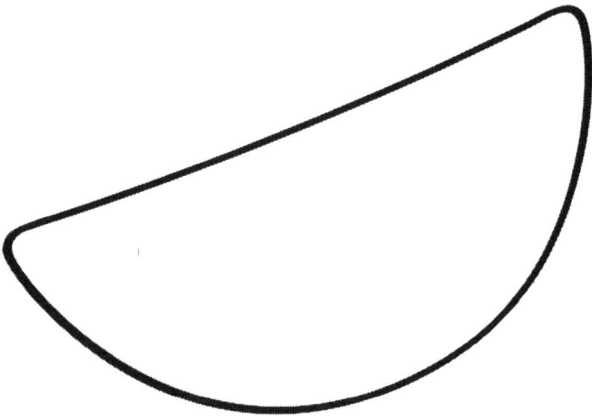

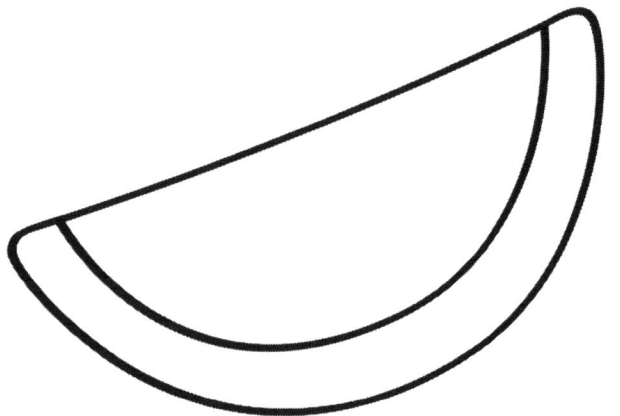

Burger

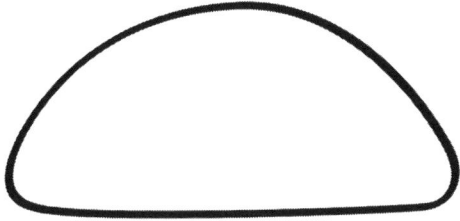
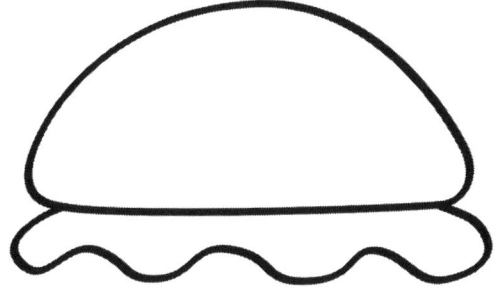

Planet

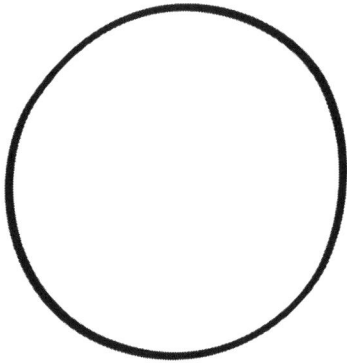
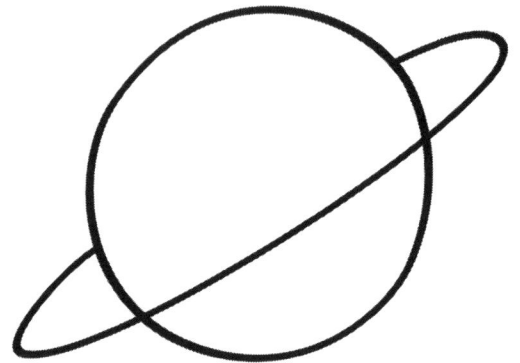
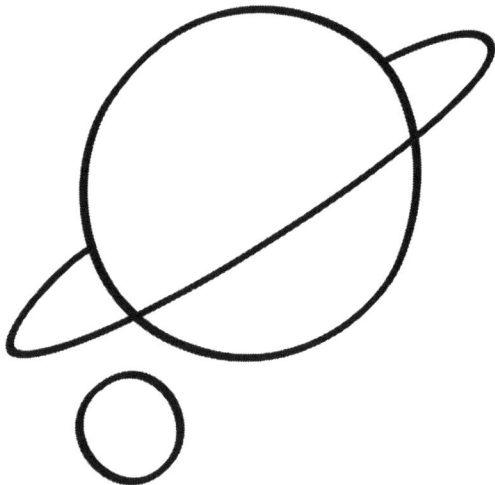

Knight

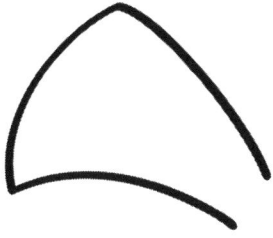
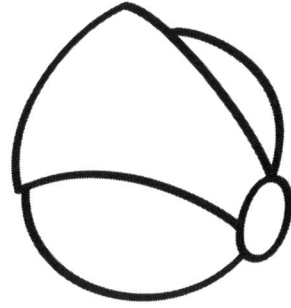

Electric Bulb

Candy Cane

UFO

Butterfly

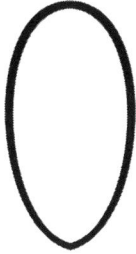
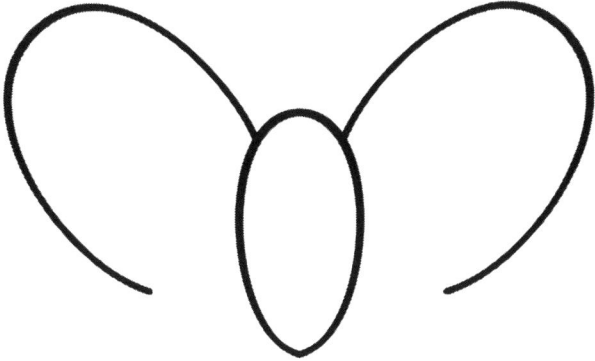

Witch

Pizza

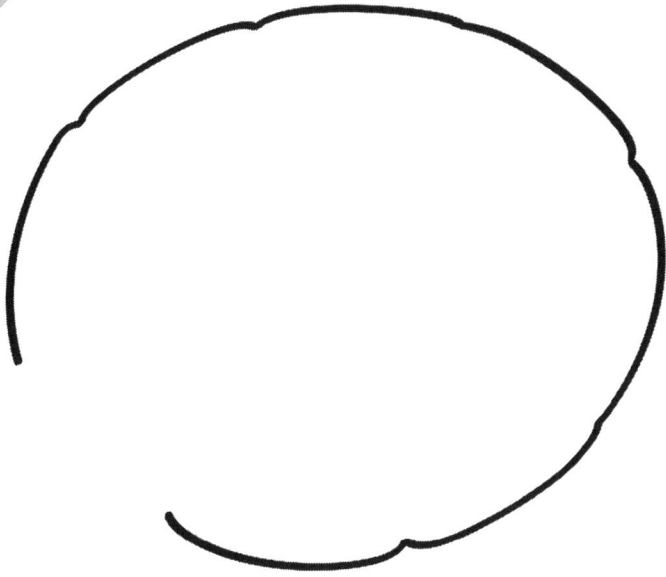
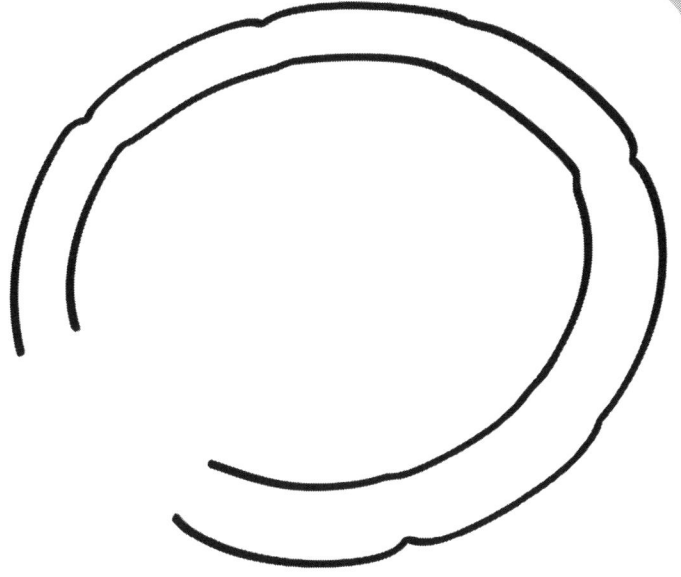
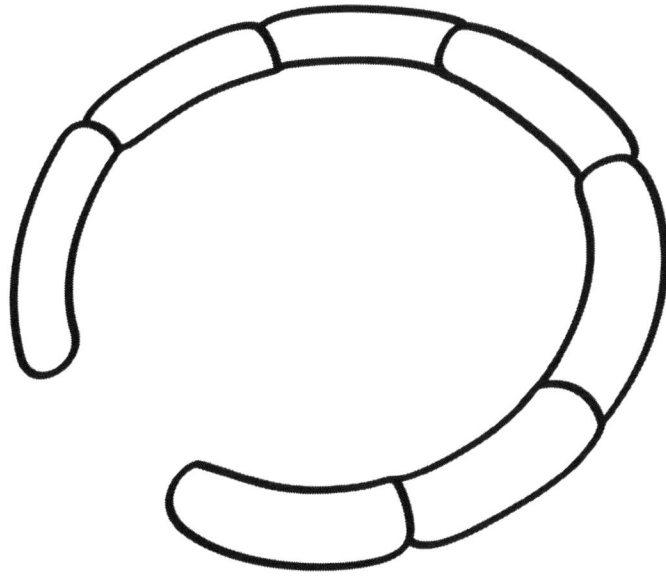
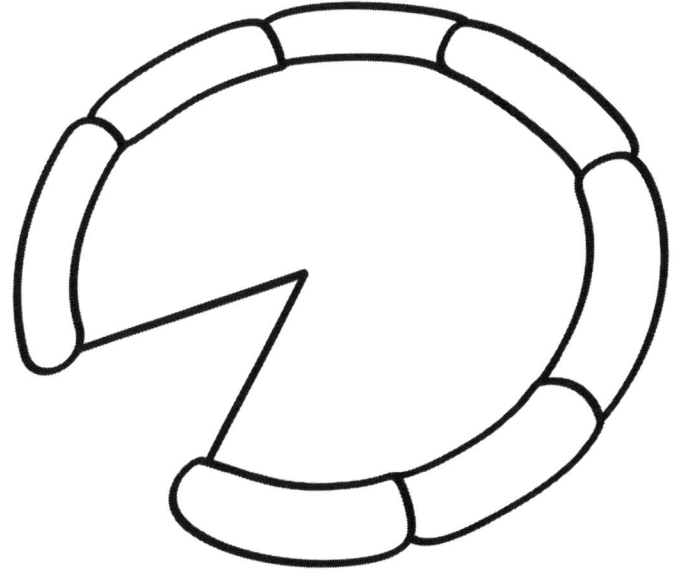
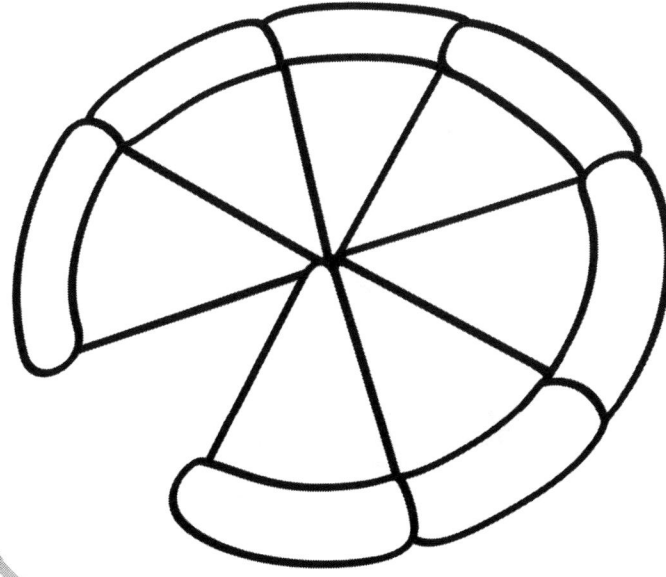

Bee

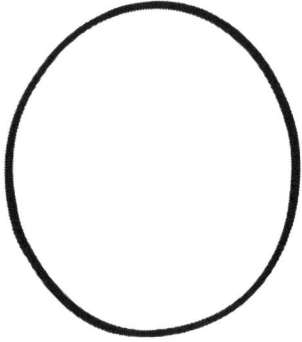
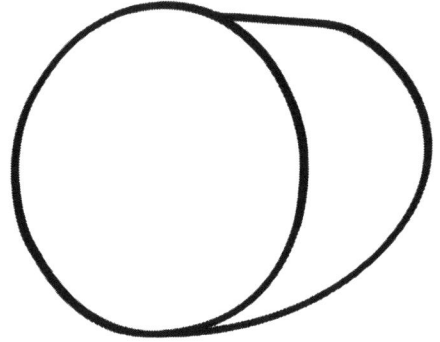

Candy

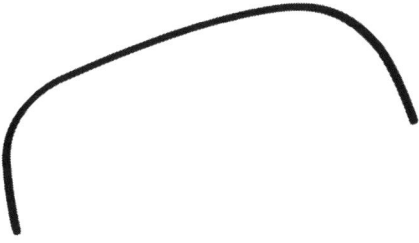
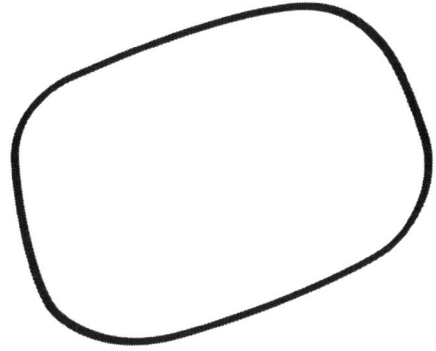

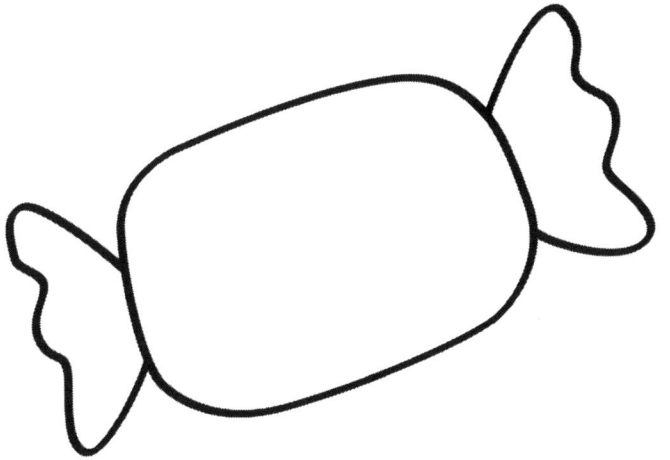

Turtle

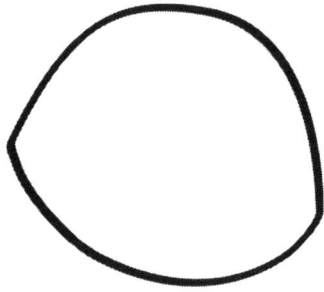
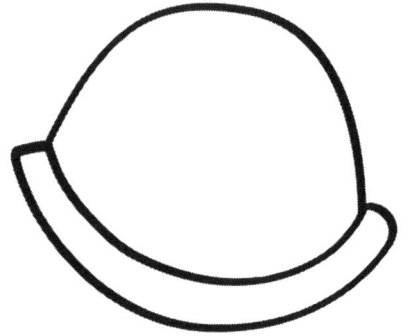
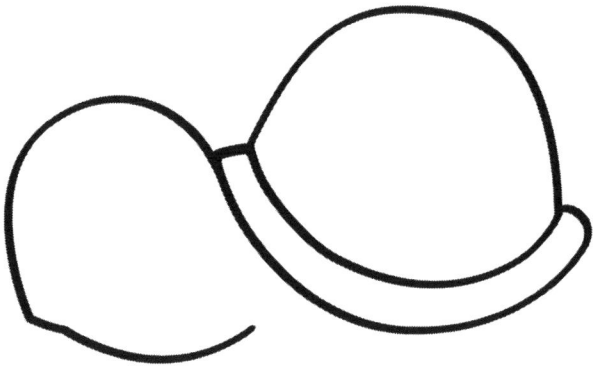

Avocado

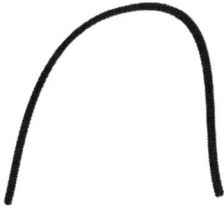
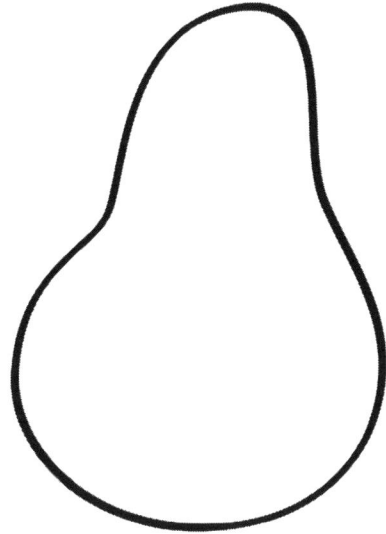
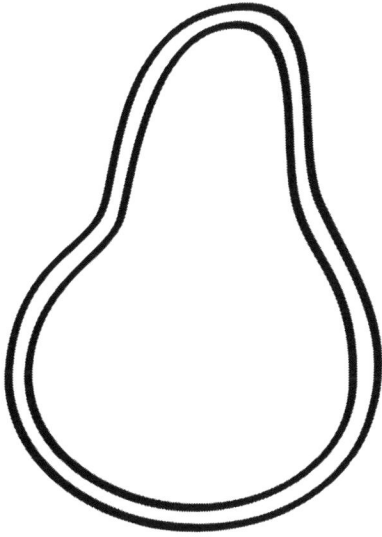
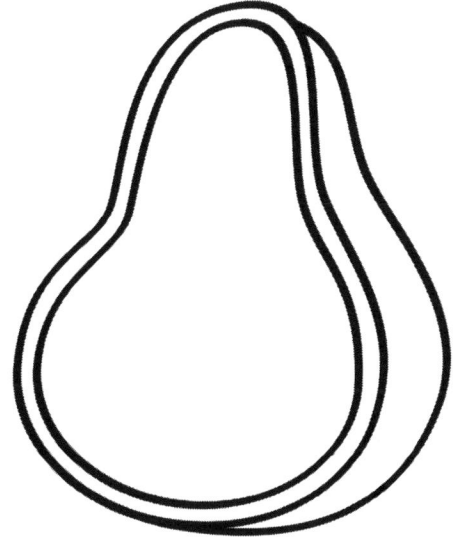
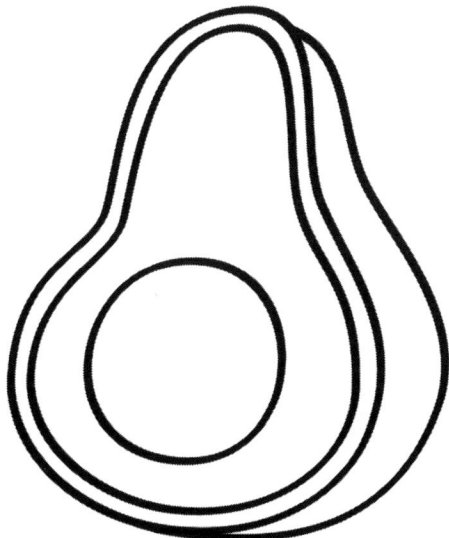
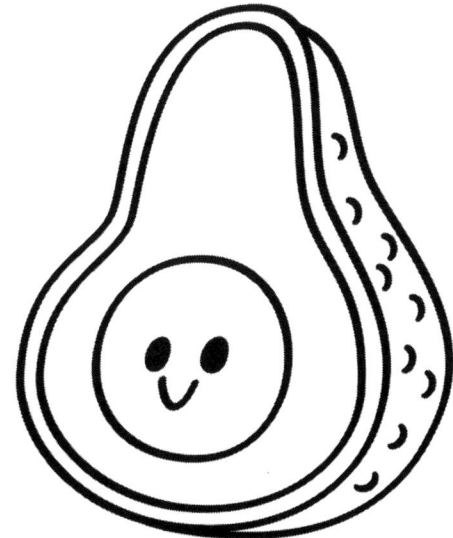

Bat

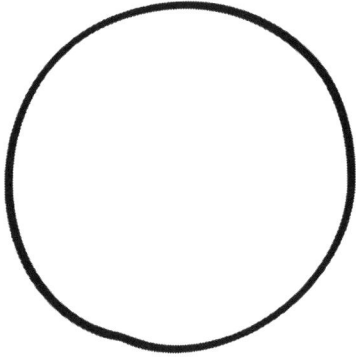

Cherry

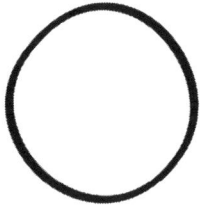
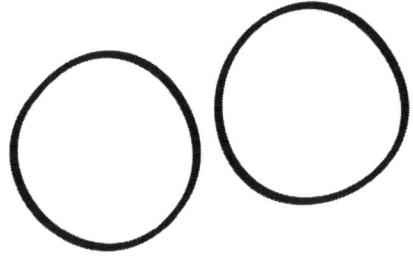

Worm

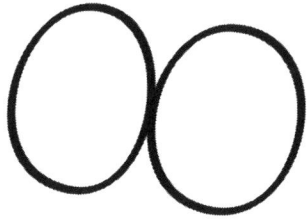
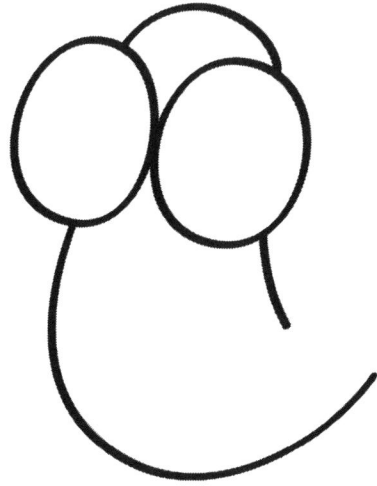

Cake Slice

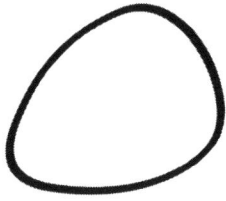 

Race Car

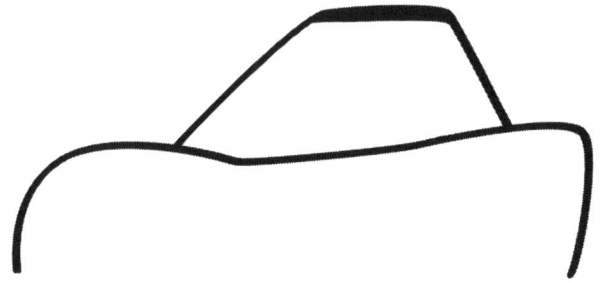

Orange

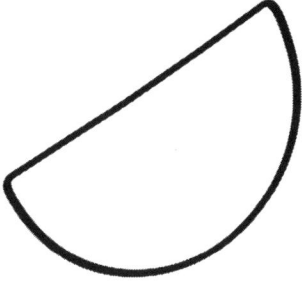
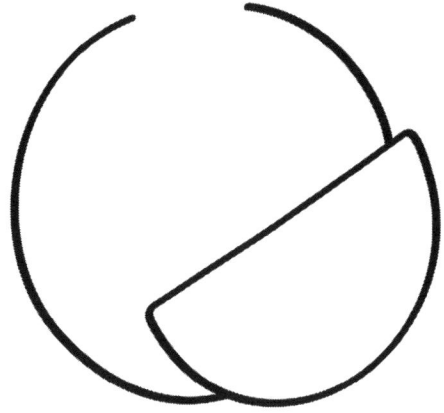
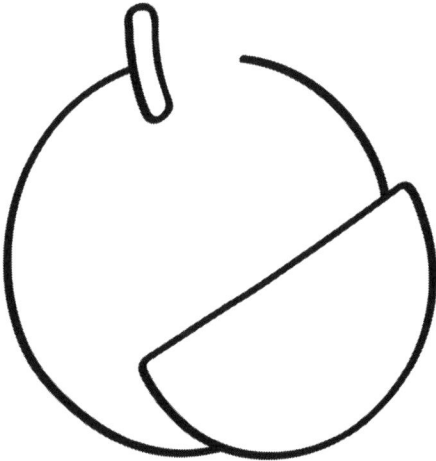

Clown

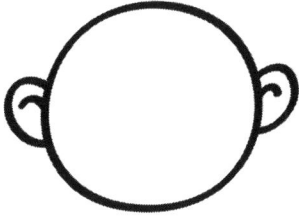

Crown

Teapot

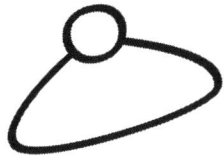

Shooting Star

Pineapple

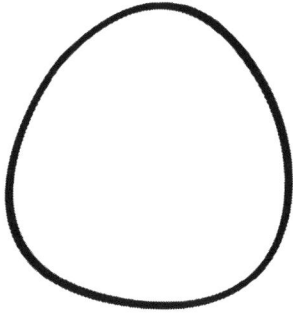

Elf

Paint Brush

 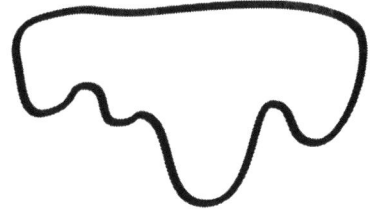

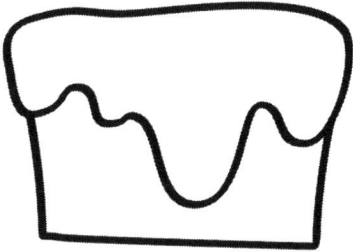 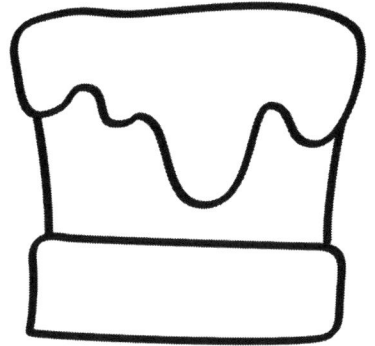

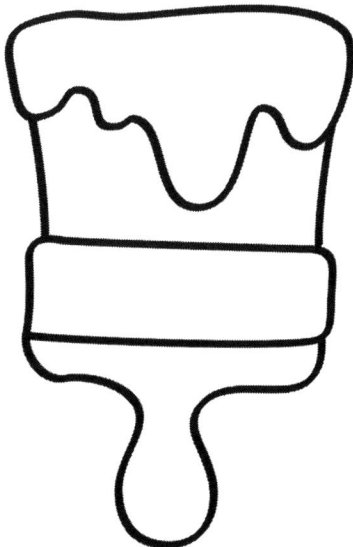 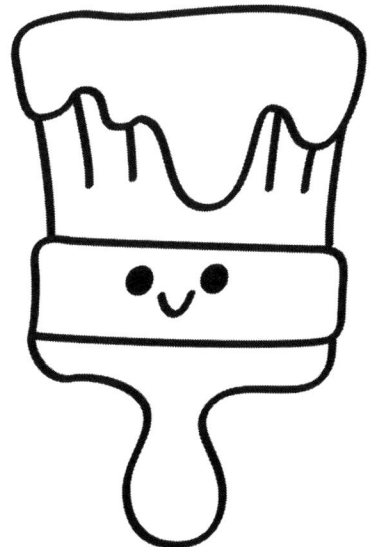

Banana

Teddy Bear

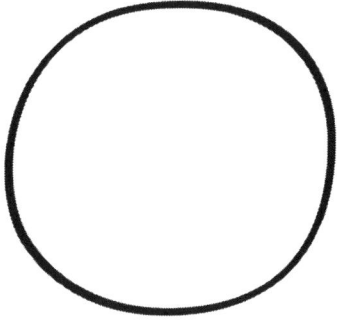
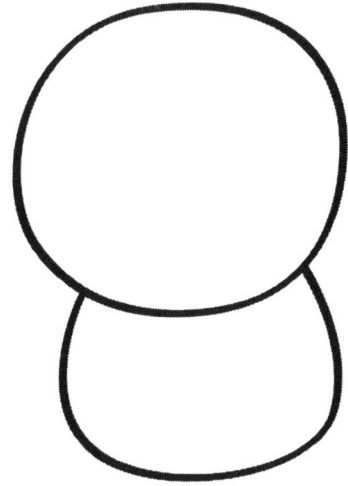
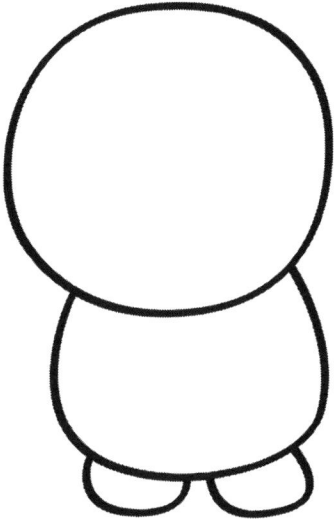

Letter

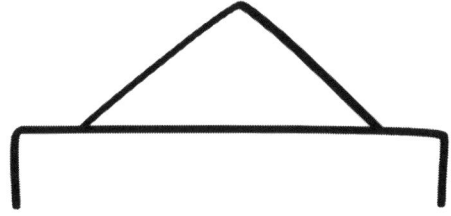

Dolphin

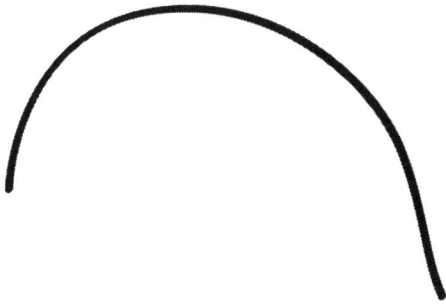
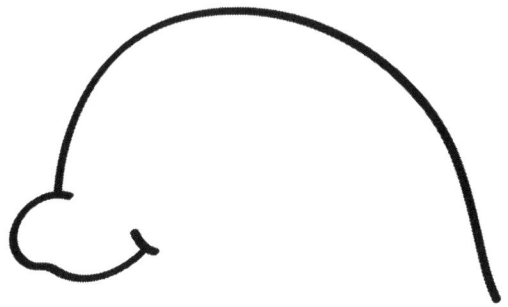

Shovel

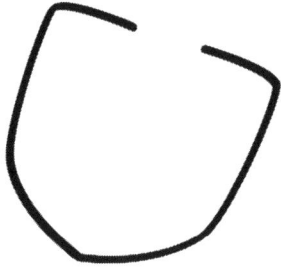

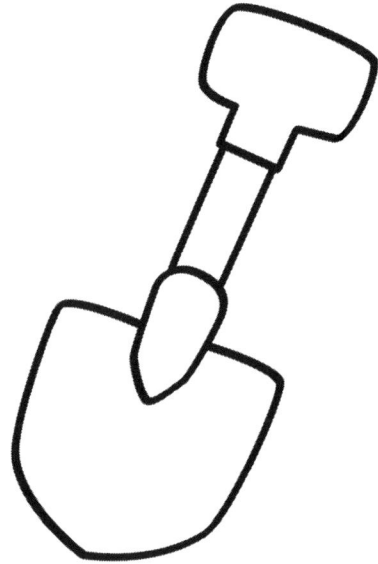

The Sun

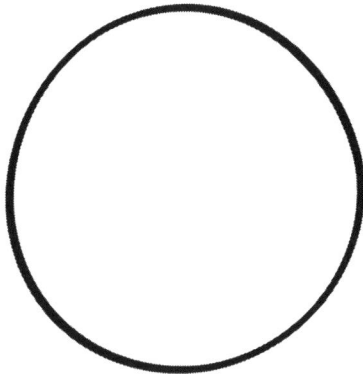

Girl

Present

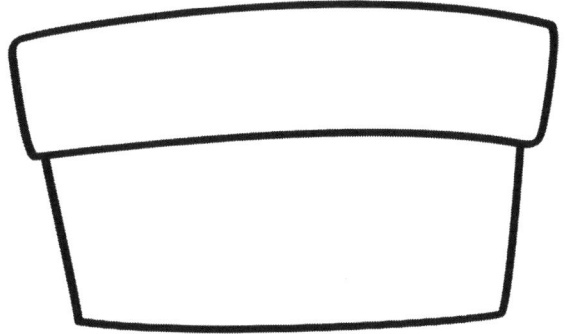
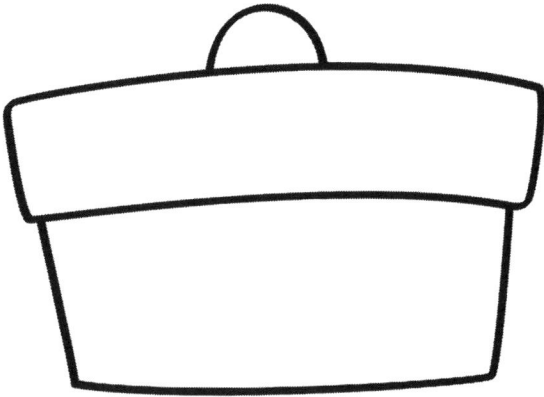

The Moon

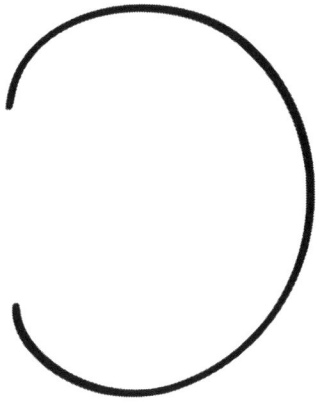

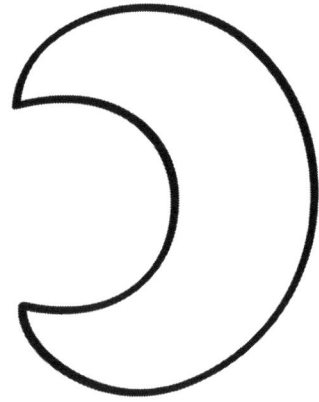

T-Shirt

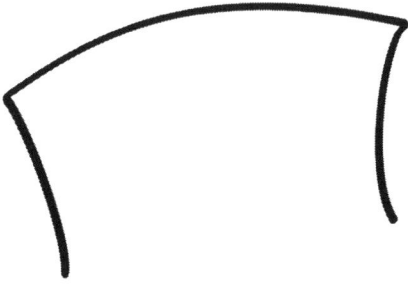

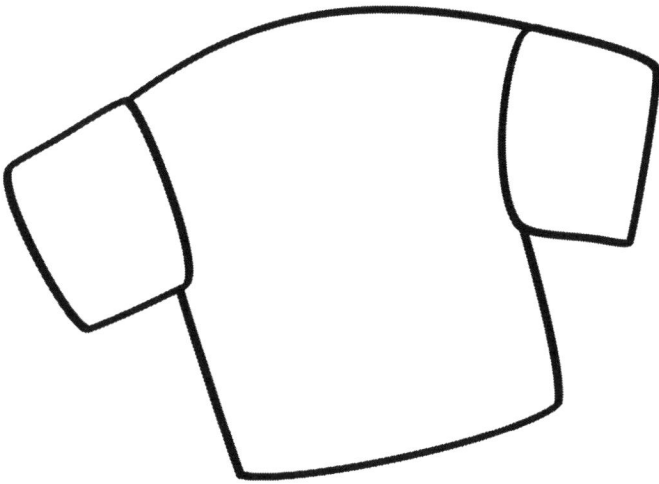
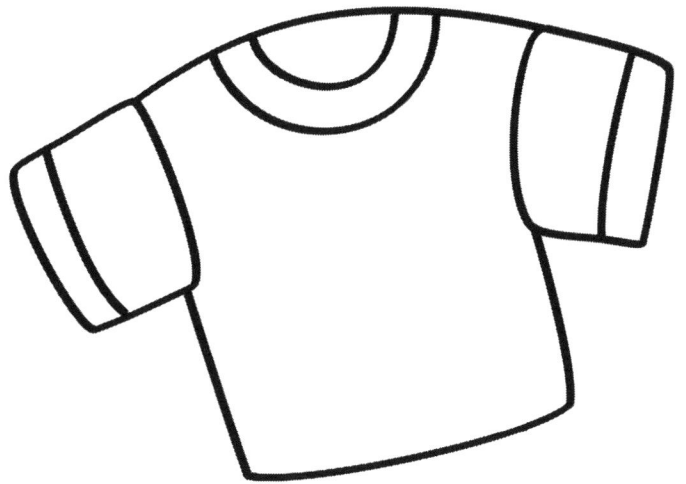
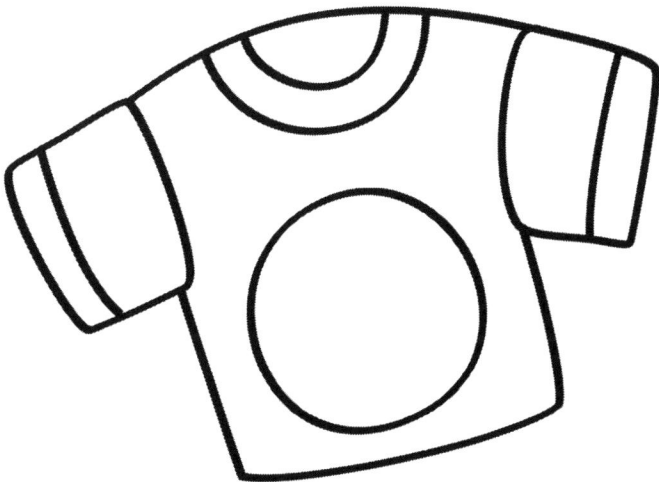

Edamame

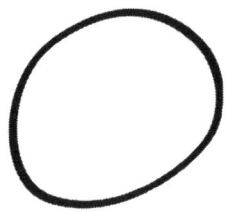
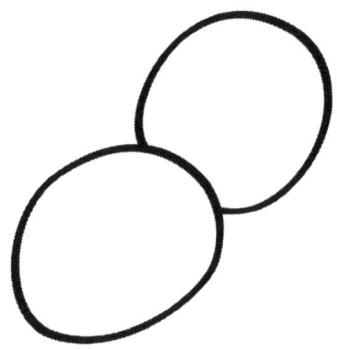
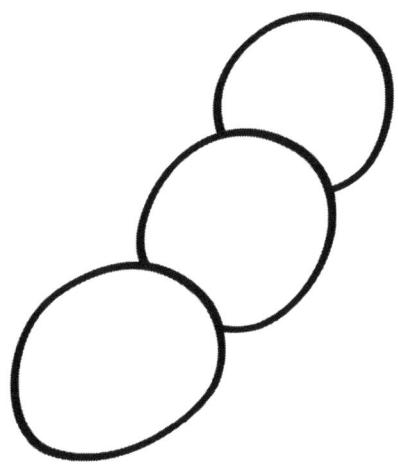
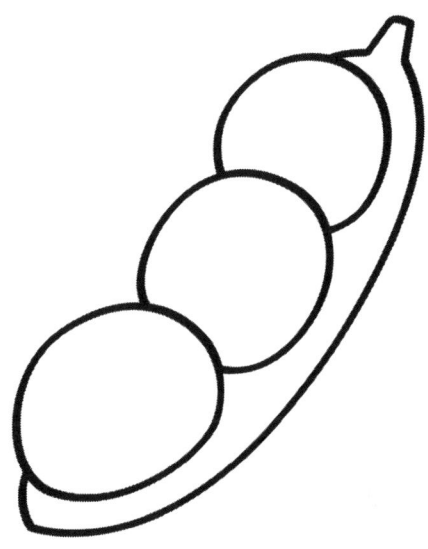
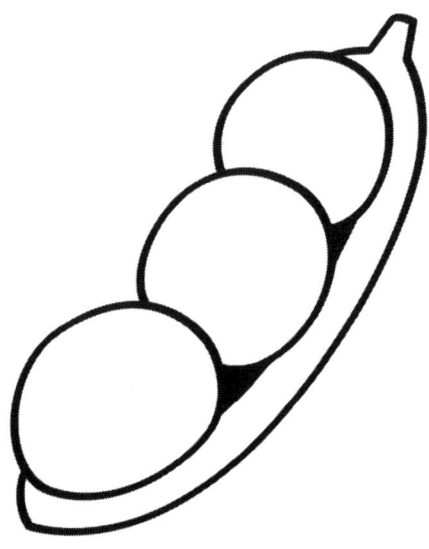

Donut

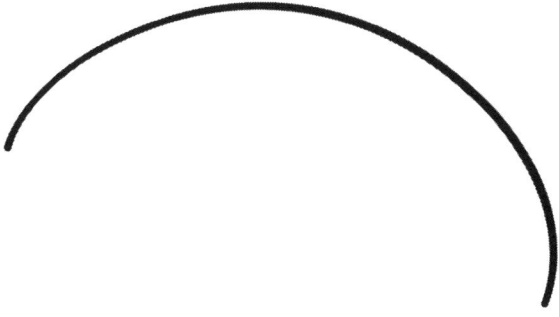 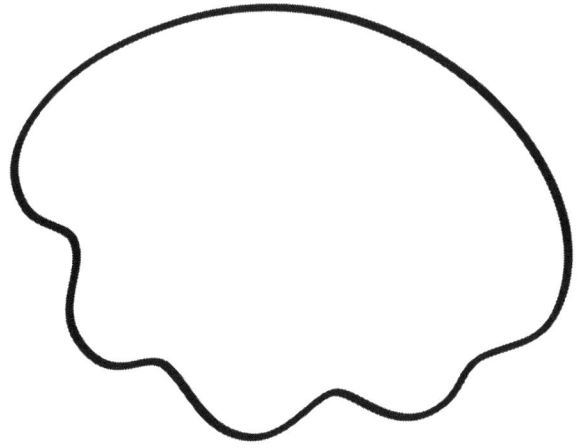

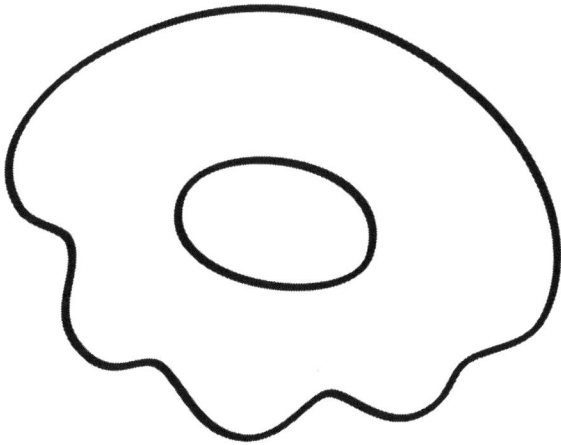 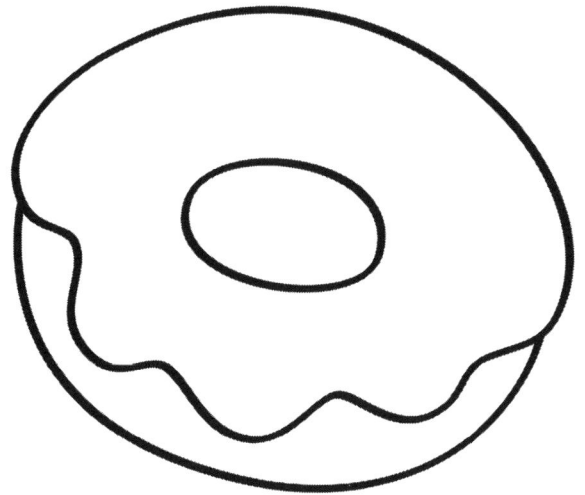

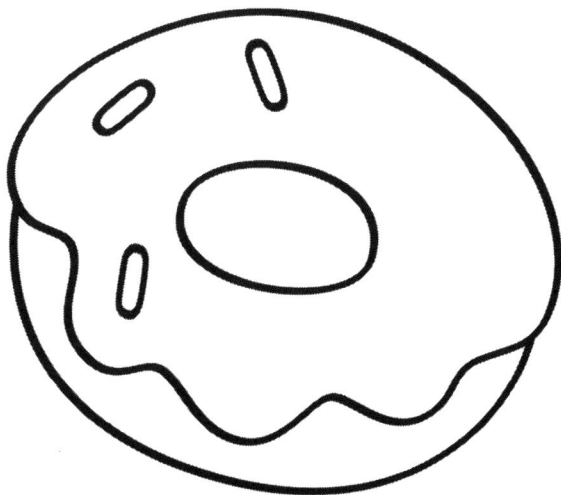 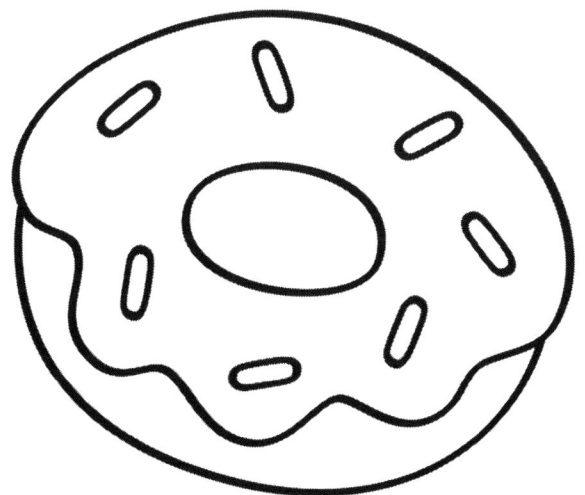

Toothbrush

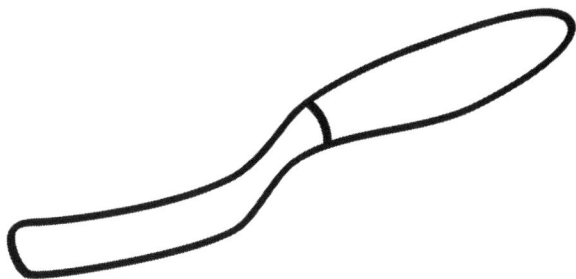

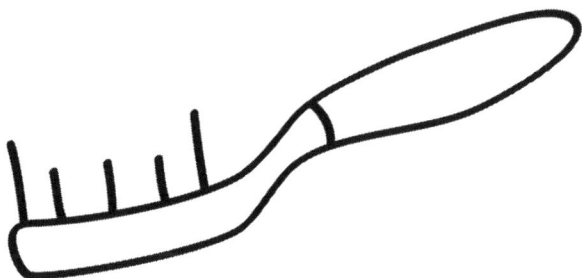

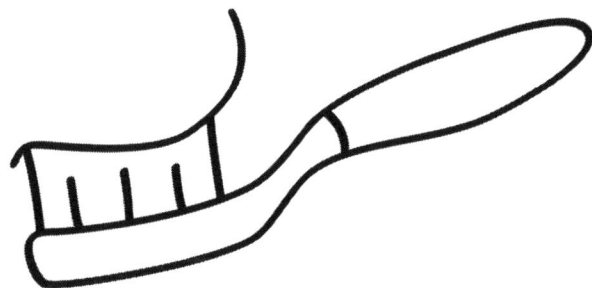

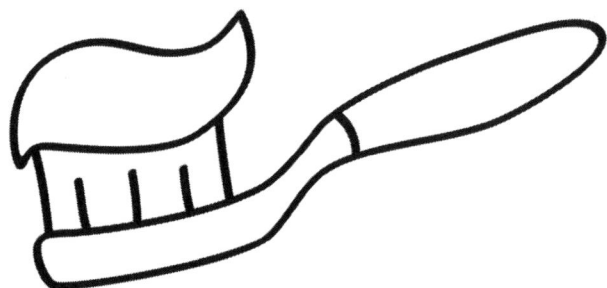

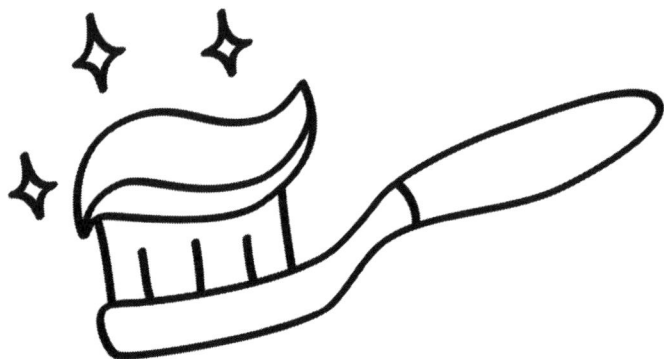

Hot Air Balloon

Owl

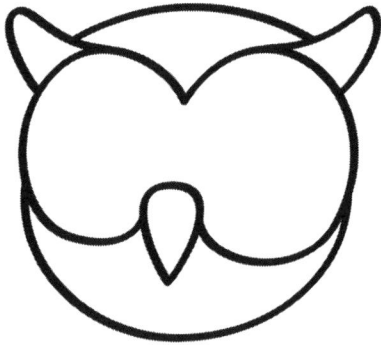
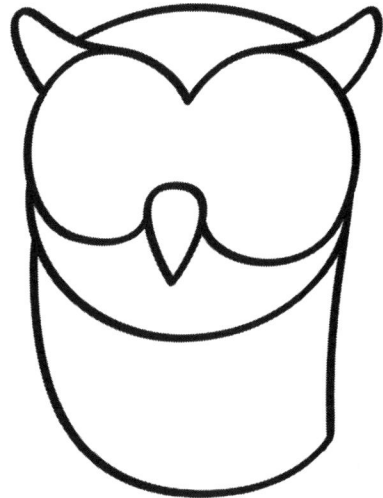

Castle

Boat

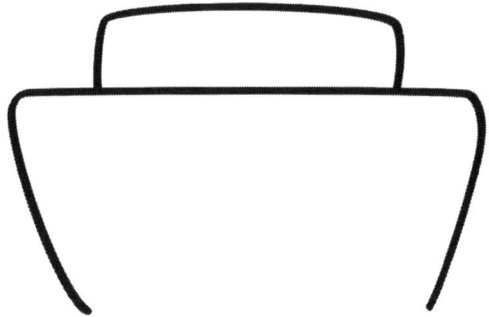

Boy

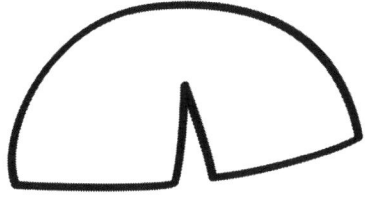

Jam Jar

 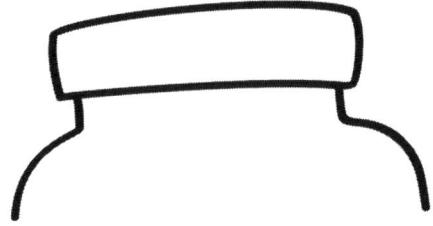

Victory Cup

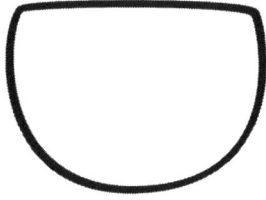

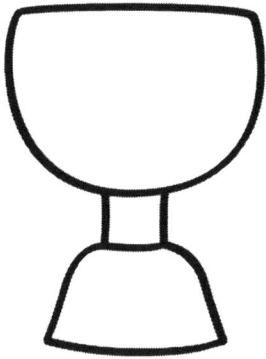

Tennis Racket

Birthday Cake

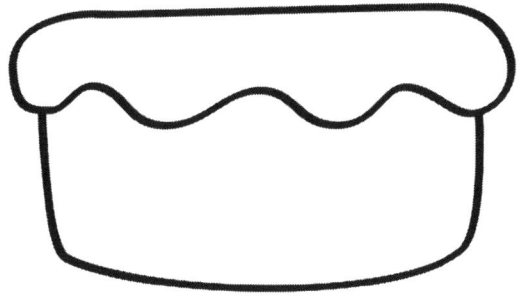

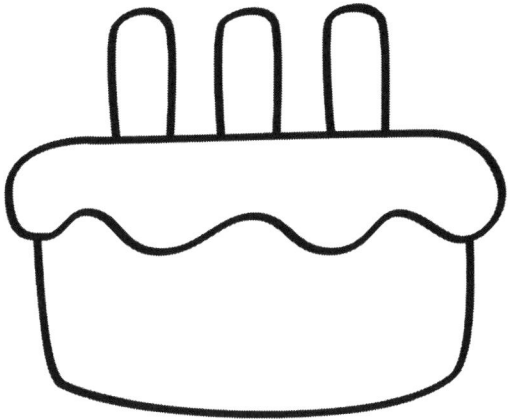

Duck Toy

Beach Hat

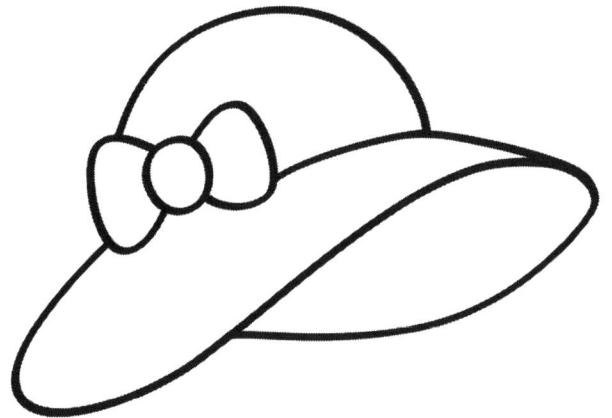

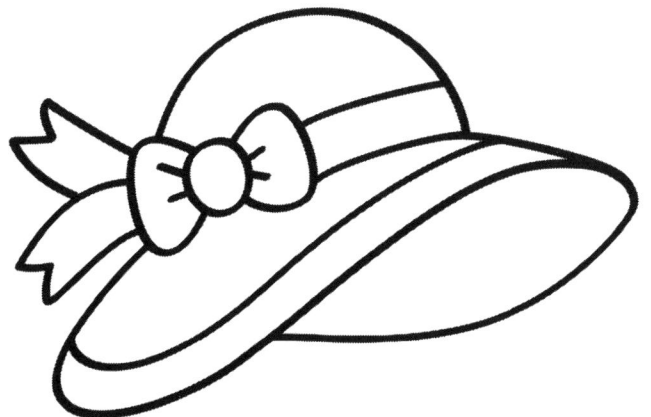

Mountain

Mouse

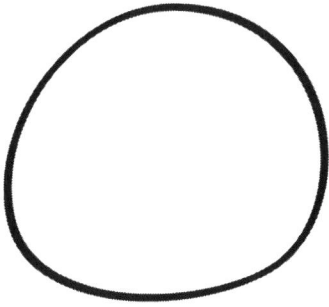
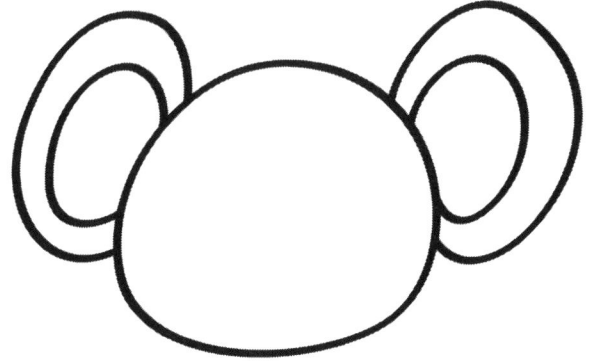

Cap

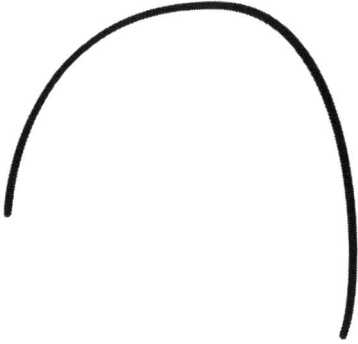
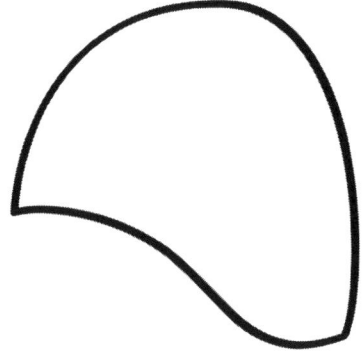
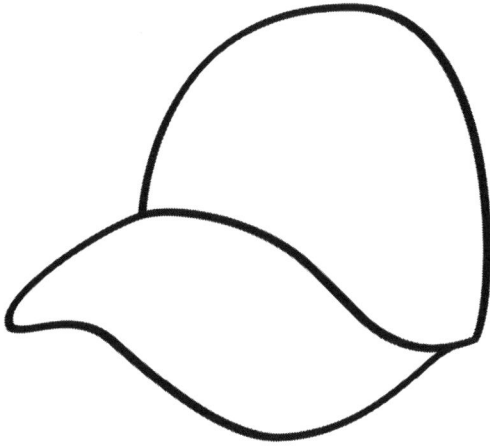

Carrot

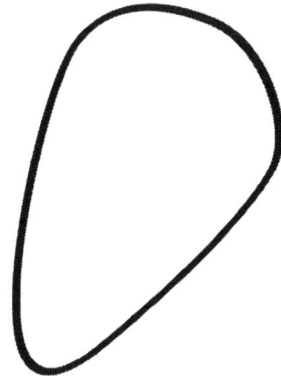
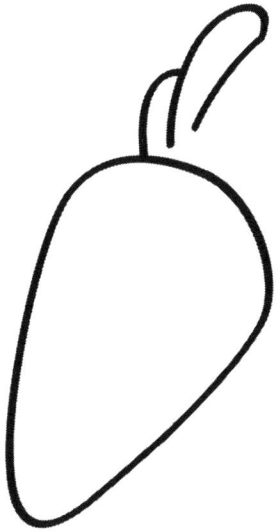
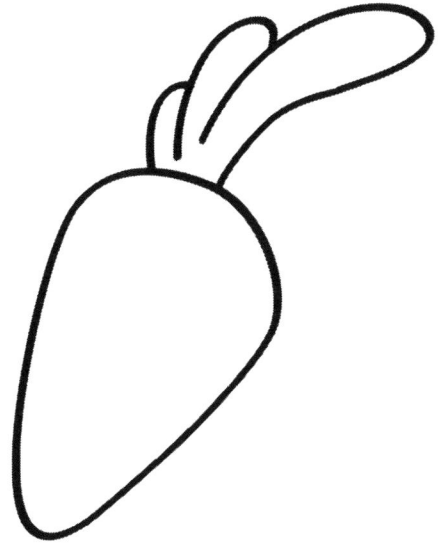

Whale

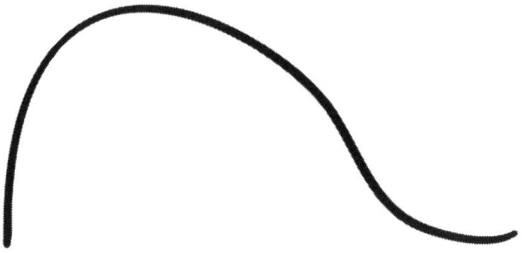

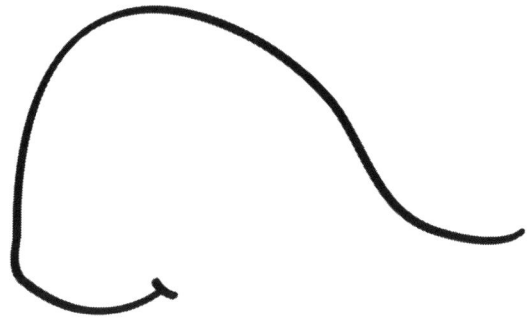

Diamond

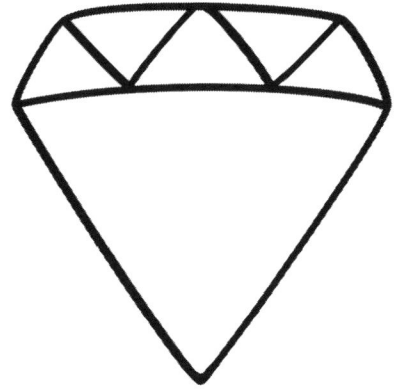

Accordion

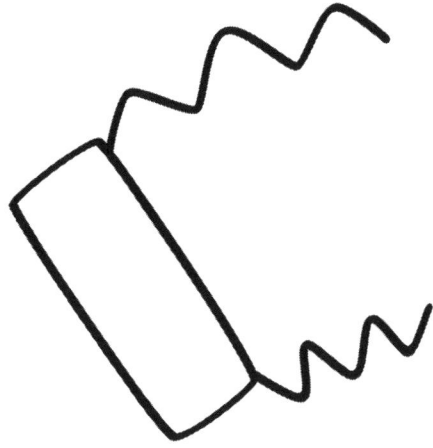

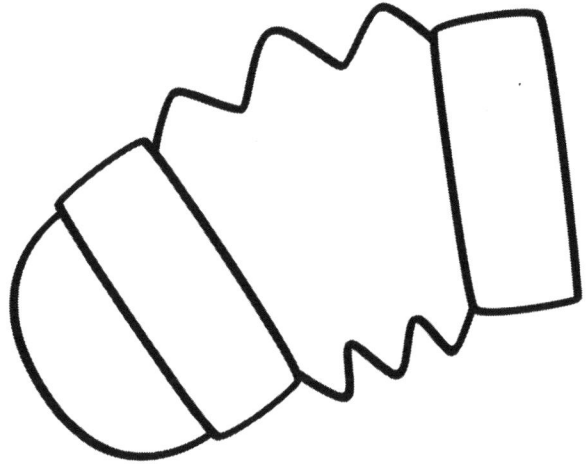
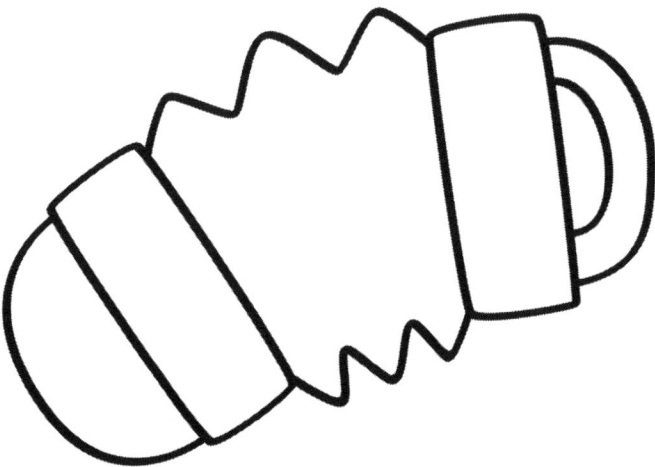

Crocodile

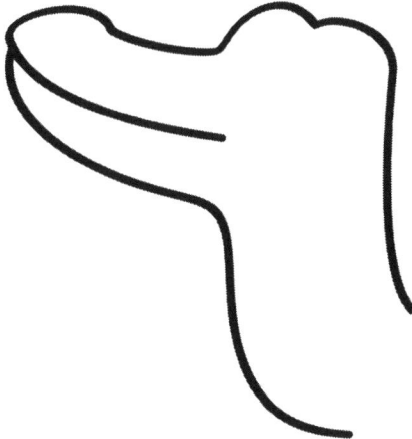

Radish

Bird

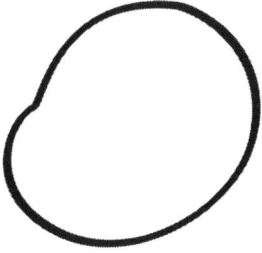
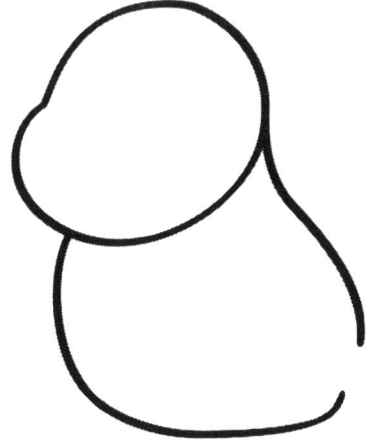
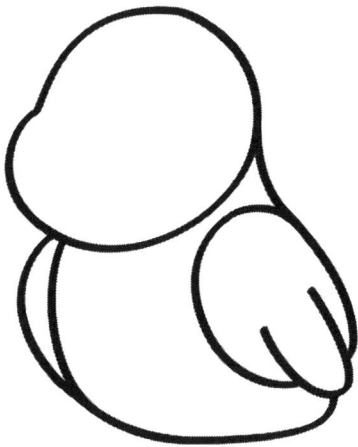
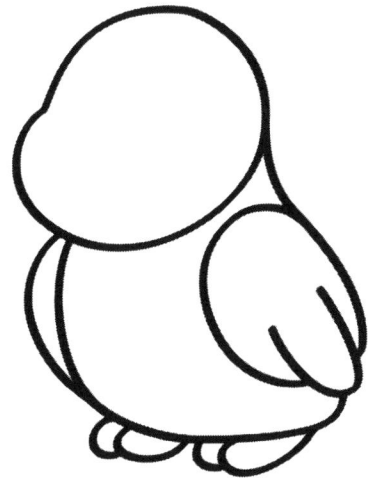

Airplane

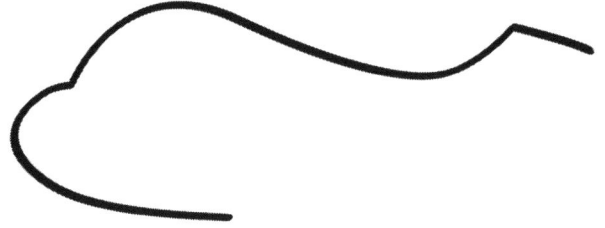
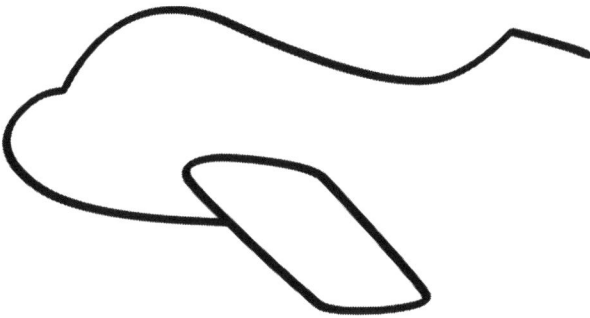
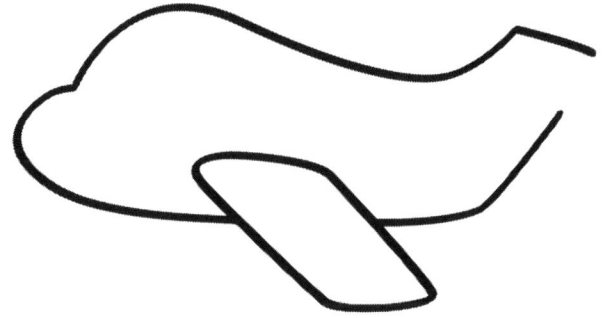
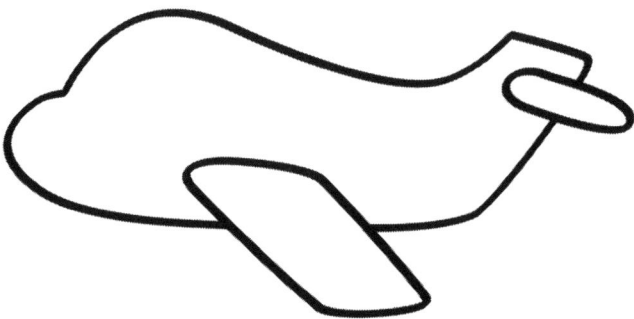

Ghost

 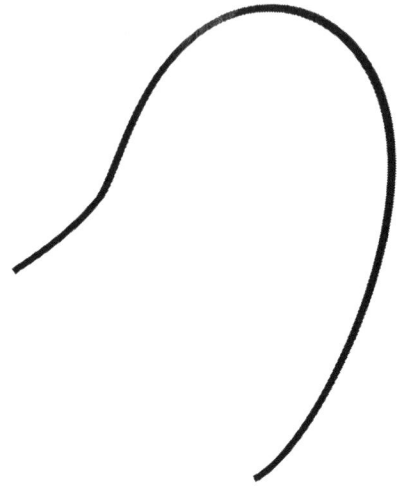

Princess

Mushroom

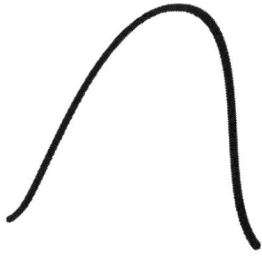
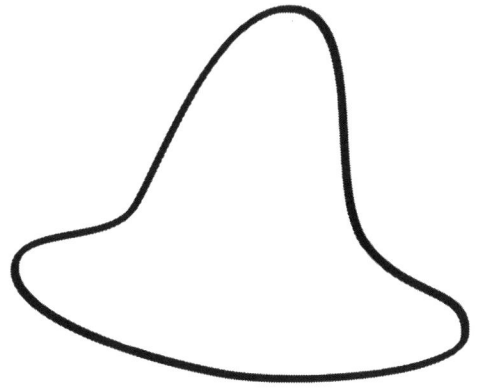

Trumpet

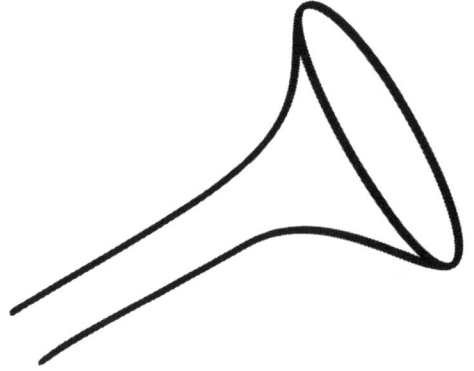

The Art Teacher

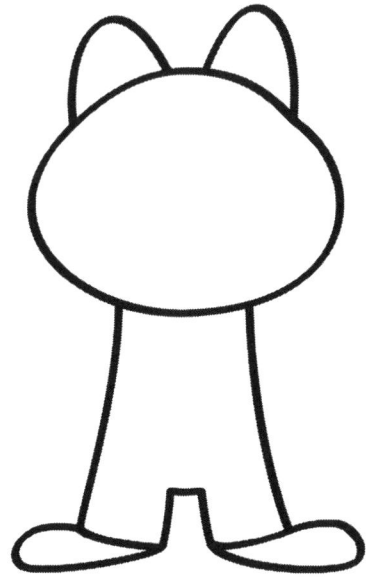

Made in United States
Troutdale, OR
10/20/2023